MW01006913

You Can

Survive

Divorce

Hope, Healing, and Encouragement
for Your Journey

JEN GRICE

GET A FREE PDF

10 Bible Truths For Reclaiming Hope During Divorce

10 BIBLE TRUTHS FOR
RECLAIMING HOPE DURING DIVORCE

He will not crush the weakest reed or put out a flickering candle. He will bring justice to all who have been wronged.
- Isaiah 42:3 NLT

The Lord is good, a strong refuge when trouble comes. He is close to those who trust in him.
- Nahum 1:7 NLT

He heals the brokenhearted and bandages their wounds.
- Psalm 147:3 NLT

"For I know the plans I have for you," says the Lord. "They are plans for good and not for disaster, to give you a future and a hope."
– Jeremiah 29:11 NLT

Don't worry about anything; instead, pray about everything. Tell God what you need, and thank him for all he has done.
- Philippians 4:6 NLT

And we know that God causes everything to work together for the good of those who love God and are called according to his purpose for them.
- Romans 8:28 NLT

Do not be afraid or discouraged, for the Lord will personally go ahead of you. He will be with you; he will neither fail you nor abandon you.
– Deuteronomy 31:8 NLT

In his kindness God called you to share in his eternal glory by means of Christ Jesus. So after you have suffered a little while, he will restore, support, and strengthen you, and he will place you on a firm foundation.
- 1 Peter 5:10 NLT

When you go through deep waters, I will be with you. When you go through rivers of difficulty, you will not drown. When you walk through the fire of oppression, you will not be burned up; the flames will not consume you.
- Isaiah 43:2 NLT

The Lord himself will fight for you. Just stay calm. - Exodus 14:14 NLT

http://jengrice.com/FreeBibleTruthsPDF

COMING SOON

You Can Survive Divorce

Bible Study

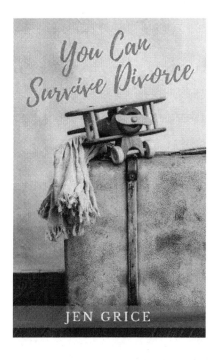

http://jengrice.com/YCSDBibleStudy

To T.J.

*Thanks for making me laugh on days I
wanted to cry.*

Grace carried me here

and by grace I'll carry on.

—Unknown

Contents

Introduction

I LOVE THE HISTORY of Joseph as told in the book of Genesis. In the years since my own divorce, Genesis 50:20 has become my life's verse: "You intended to harm me, but God intended it all for good. He brought me to this position so I could save the lives of many people." Sometimes God brings us through some pretty bad experiences, including a rotten marriage or a difficult divorce, not to harm us, but because He plans to use our lives to save others.

That is Joseph's story. It is mine as well. Nothing that I've gone through happened in vain. What should have harmed me and left me bitter and angry has made me more dependent on God and my faith in His promises. Now I look for ways to use everything for good. I walk redeemed, and I share my story here so others can as well. I do not sugarcoat my own story or pretend it was easy. Like Joseph, I struggled. I spent nights crying out to God for mercy. I felt so very alone, and oftentimes I actually was. I share the raw truths with you because they are part of my story, just as much as the end results.

Joseph had a dream that his brothers would bow down to him someday, but God never told Joseph what he would have to endure while he waited. For twenty-two years he struggled, yet his integrity never wavered. He never wallowed in self-pity or schemed up ways to escape his circumstances. Instead he held tightly to that dream of a new identity given to him by God while giving his best in all that he did, no matter where he was. He was anointed for just such a purpose. *Oh, if only it were so easy to read about Joseph's anointed life once and keep the faith ourselves in the darkness of divorce.*

Thankfully God doesn't expect us to carry our burdens on our own. Paul told us to share in each other's burdens as a way to obey the law of Christ (Galatians 6:2). When we feel weighed down or crushed by the weight of it all, hearing someone else's story of survival and eventual state of thriving can bring us hope, if we let it. That's my plan for this book.

If you are newly separated, going through a divorce, or recently divorced, I want to encourage you today with hope that you can survive after divorce. Like Joseph, we have no idea of the trials we will face in the future, or when we'll have to flee from sin, but we can be sure that God keeps His promises and will never abandon us.

> *We are pressed on every side by troubles, but we are not crushed. We are perplexed, but not driven to despair. We are hunted down, but never abandoned by God. We get knocked down, but we are not destroyed. Through suffering, our bodies continue to share in the death of Jesus so that the life of Jesus may also be seen in our bodies.*
>
> —2 Corinthians 4:8–10

Friend, I've been knocked down, I've felt the pressures from all sides, and it felt like I might be destroyed by it all. Divorce is a tough-as-nails season of life, but I'm here to tell you I've survived. You can too, and your life may even be better for it. I have faith in you as you journey through your season of divorce, that the path before you will bring you to a better place for you and your children. I have faith in the One who allows divorce to happen, faith that there is some greater purpose in all of this, and that someday we shall all see it.

1

Accept God' s Healing

He heals the brokenhearted and bandages their wounds.

—Psalm 147:3

ALTHOUGH A FEW PEOPLE told me I should be rejoicing in my freedom from the oppression I had been dealing with for so long, all I felt was despair at the end of my marriage. I knew in my head I never wanted to go back, but my heart was still very broken. I was a jumbled mess of hurt, fear, confusion, and hopelessness, and I thought my life was completely over. I was so stressed. My life was complete chaos. And I wasn't sure how I'd survive as a single parent. I hadn't worked outside the home in well over a decade. I had just a few months before the kids and I needed to be out of the marital home, all while having a court order saying I was to continue homeschooling my youngest child. The future was so unsure and mostly seemed dark.

I would cry out to God to guide me. When I didn't hear back, I felt anger. Most times I just wanted answers and clear guidance, but I felt and heard nothing. I felt so unloved and uncared for. Maybe God had abandoned me too. Maybe God sided with my husband. All of my despair surrounded me and wanted to pull me under. I knew turning to drugs, alcohol, or another man was not the quick-fix bandage I was looking for. I knew that was just a good way to lose custody of my kids or make things much worse, but I had no idea where I could turn to get rid of all of the hurt. Where could I turn with all of the hemorrhaging pain? Who would heal me?

We often hear that time is the healer of our pain, but I don't believe that is true. I've met women decades after their divorces, still holding tightly to their hurts and trapped in their pain. So no, time does not hold the healing power that helps us embrace the future. Time does nothing but keep going.

We cannot bypass the process by using the world's comforts. That only delays the process and often sets us back, because we add more pain we have to then face, once we finally deal with it. Grief is just put on hold when trying to "move on" while still healing. Not only does taking baggage into a new relationship hurt the relationship, but after that rebound relationship ends, the already hurting heart is hurting ten times more. So where do we start with healing? Healing or not healing depends on the source. And there is only one person who can do the job. God is our creator and healer. It's what He calls Himself.

Our "Jehovah Rapha"

If you will listen carefully to the voice of the Lord your God and do what is right in his sight, obeying his commands and keeping all his decrees, then I will not make you suffer any of the diseases I sent on the Egyptians;

*for **I am the Lord who heals you.***

—Exodus 15:26, emphasis mine

The Hebrew word *rapha* means to heal or restore, so God's name, Jehovah Rapha, means "I am the Lord who heals." He heals His beloved daughters' physical, emotional, and spiritual wounds. Nothing here on earth can replace a healing from our creator. For a short time, Jesus walked the earth sharing His healing power. In Mark 5, we read the story of a woman who lived with a bleeding disorder. Time was not her healer. Doctors were only making her worse as the decades passed. She must have felt so much shame and loss of hope with her condition, much like we often feel after divorce. I know I felt like I was emotionally hemorrhaging every time I left the house. Can you imagine it actually being physical? My tears were enough to scare people away from me on Sunday mornings.

Then the woman heard of Jesus's healing powers and kind, gentle spirit from the men who saw Him performing miracles, and they experienced His healing too. How brave of her to set aside her shame to leave her house, full of a tiny new tendril of hope that this Jesus man could heal her too. She had a desire to be healed that day, trusting God had sent her a healer.

She knew her source.

When Jesus got off the boat, this woman saw a large crowd around Him. I imagine she thought, *Maybe if I could get close to Him. What if I just touched His robe?* She wanted badly to be healed, so she went straight to the source to get it. And at that very moment, she trusted that she would be healed.

And that's exactly what happened. As she touched Jesus, He felt the healing power leave Him. Then He told her, "Daughter, your faith has made you well. Go in peace. Your suffering is over." (Mark 5:34) What a miraculous story of God's healing power poured out through Jesus. Even though Jesus no longer walks this earth, His healing is still here and available for all who desire it, believe it, and have faith in Him. That's where we start the healing process.

The Eternal Healer

> *You are blessed because you believed that the Lord would do what he said.*
>
> —Luke 1:45

The Lord promises healing to all who come to Him seeking it. He wants to take all your pain, all your hurts, and all the difficulties you face and bandage them up; and his healing is not just a quick fix, but a whole heart and soul healing. He wants to apply His healing salve and nurse you back to health. Even better, He plans to restore you. Yes, this takes time. But yet again, time is not your healer, God is. This won't be a one-time healing transformation like the one the hemorrhaging woman (mentioned in Mark 5) received. But if you keep bringing your wounds to Him for healing, He promises to make you well. He wants to restore, support, and strengthen you. He wants to make you into something more beautiful than before.

> *In his kindness God called you to share in his eternal glory by means of Christ Jesus. So after you have suffered a little while, he will restore, support, and strengthen you, and he will place you on a firm foundation.*

—1 Peter 5:10

Healing is a gift from God. He asks for nothing more than your complete faith that He can and will heal your heart. He will then protect your heart and guide you all the rest of your days on earth, through the Holy Spirit. Always seek Him first. It's the only relationship you can put 100 percent of your trust in. He's committed to loving you like no other man in your life. He's devoted to you. He will never leave you or abandon you. He's always with you.

Your Most Important Relationship

> *Come, let us worship and bow down. Let us kneel before the Lord our maker, for he is our God. We are the people he watches over, the flock under his care. If only you would listen to his voice today!*
>
> —Psalm 95:6–7

It is so much easier to put tangible things first in our lives. Our jobs are important because they provide money to pay the bills. Our kids (or fur babies) are important because they depend on us to feed and care for them. Their neediness often makes it hard to even put ourselves first, let alone any other relationship.

But God is a jealous God. He wants to be at the center of your world. He wants you to worship Him above anything or anyone else, so much so that He may even remove people or things that stand in the way of your relationship with Him. He's been known to take women out of a relationship that is unhealthy. He wants better for His precious daughters. He wants to have a close relationship with you and for you to worship Him above all else. He knows what's best, and holding onto anything tighter than you're holding on to God is not healthy for you. Just as it's impossible for any relationship to grow without talking to that person, or investing your time in that relationship, you need to devote time to being with God. Spend time getting to know Him and learn what He says in His Word. Not fully understanding God's Word and His promises allowed me to feel unloved and unworthy of love, but after working on my relationship with God, I was able to find my worth in Him. Now I know I am loved and I'll never feel lonely again, even when I am alone.

God also wants you to spend time speaking to Him through prayer. You'll need Him the most during your biggest trials and hurts, but you can forget He's right there for you when things are okay.

He hasn' t left you.

Call out to Him. He is right next to you, keeping watch over you with care. When can you schedule time with your heavenly Father? What can you do on a daily and weekly basis to build your relationship with Him? When can you find time to worship, pray, study, and fellowship with other believers? When can you spend time praising Him for all He has done? As a single, work-at-home mom, I have to carve out time for God. I have to be very intentional about it, as sometimes I forget. It's important to me to put God first in my life, in front of everything and everyone else, because I didn't always do that. At one point, I even found myself worshipping a man on earth rather than my creator.

If you don't have a regular habit of reading the Bible, today is the best time to start. God's Word will heal you and show you the way to restoration in your life. He wants to give you hope, peace, and a brighter future.

God Heals and Restores

My healing has taken years and still continues to this day. Some of the hard feelings still pop up on occasion, but I'm not emotionally bleeding like I was in the beginning. It was my time spent reading, learning, and growing in my relationship with my Father that helped get me through. This also helped me to put Him back to the center of my life, right where He belongs. I know that wouldn't have happened if I was still a married woman. I know God rescued me from my misplaced worship. My friend, no one and nothing are going to heal this pain but our Lord. Healing is not one-dimensional; it's multi-dimensional. At the center should be God. He wants to heal you and restore you, the way He did me. He doesn't want you to be in bondage to your pain any longer. There is freedom in acknowledging the wrongs, experiencing the feelings, and working through the forgiveness over time.

It's not a 1-2-3-done process.

There will be lots of starts and stops as you journey through this healing. Some days you'll feel like you're back at step one. You may even hit stumbling blocks that snag you into going in the wrong direction. But all in all, God is the secret to getting back up, and day by day, what you thought might kill you may make you a little stronger. It may also make you a lot more dependent on God. Sometimes that is all part of

JEN GRICE

His plan: to bring you back to Him, right where you belong. God is still in the restoration business, and He has plans to heal and restore you. Your only job is to put your faith in Him and trust Him with the rest.

Keep the Faith

> *Faith shows the reality of what we hope for; it is the evidence of things we cannot see. Through their faith, the people in days of old earned a good reputation.*
>
> —Hebrews 11:1–2

Often during divorce we feel like we may have lost our faith. We wonder what God is doing and why He allows such horrible things to happen. As we walk through the valley, we wonder if we're all alone.

But speaking from the other side of this painful experience, I can see where my faith has brought me safely through the valley. Faith is knowing something good can, and will, come out of something bad.

Jesus personified and became our hope. Our Savior. Something good that came out of something bad. We see other examples of this in

God's Word. Again, Joseph's life has been one such example that I have found hope in. We can read about his struggles and loads of seemingly unneeded pain, but we see in the end that God worked it all out for good.

> *And we know that God causes everything to work together for the good of those who love God and are called according to His purpose for them.*
>
> —Romans 8:28

I share my story to give the same hope to those who read my blog, watch my YouTube videos, or read my books. I like to think of it as being a lighthouse to those who are crashing into the same rocks I just traveled through. I'm on the other side, safe and sound, waving for you to follow in this direction. Just like many divorced women before you, you can get through this.

As hard as these words are to accept right now, God has made His promises and He plans to keep them. Your faith in Him and His promises will be your light at the end of this dark tunnel.

At the end of this book is a link to a printable sheet of ten Bible verses on my blog to keep you encouraged. When your faith gets shaky, read the

Word to remind yourself God's promises are true for you; you just need to remind yourself to keep the faith.

The Importance of Heart Healing

In my experience, in talking with people who have divorced more than once, most think that because their divorce was their "spouse's fault," they'll do better the next time they get married. This line of thinking is usually quite false. Many jump into dating too quickly without healing and dealing with their own issues first. I've seen countless women remarry only to divorce a second time shortly thereafter. This is because unhealthy people are drawn to unhealthy people. If you were in an unhealthy relationship in the past, the chances of getting into another unhealthy relationship are much higher. We gravitate toward what we know to be "normal."

If you spend your time looking for someone new instead of working on your healing, you may end up with the same person you were married to—just in a different body. The better alternative is to take the time to really heal your heart so that when God brings someone healthy your way, you'll be prepared and know the difference between healthy and unhealthy. It's much easier for a healthy person to see the red flags than a hurting person.

Work through all of the pain, deal with your past, figure out why you married the type of person you married (even if he changed during the marriage), and learn all that you can so that you don't become someone's next target. I want to see you have a healthy future, whether that means you stay single or remarry, but both paths must include the deep heart healing and cleansing only God can provide.

He loves you too much to see you in another miserable marriage. And if He allowed you to escape from oppression the first time, He doesn't want to see you go back to that same situation again. Trust Him to guide you into this new chapter of life. Allow Him to be your husband during this season. He is your hope, your healer, your redeemer and "by his wounds you are healed" (1 Peter 2:24).

Don't allow pain to be your lifetime partner.

Your Father is ready to take that place. Keep the faith and allow Him to heal you.

Give Yourself Grace

So let us come boldly to the throne of our gracious God. There we will receive his mercy, and we will find grace to help us when we need it most.

—Hebrews 4:16

I have to honestly say that healing doesn't always look so pretty. During your healing, don't worry about doing it perfectly, because there is no such thing. I haven't known one divorced woman who made healing look beautiful. But what I have seen done well is when a woman gives herself grace and mercy to heal exactly the way God needs her to heal, in the time that God has set aside for her to heal. I believe God wants to use all the bad we've experienced in our lives to minister to others. When we share in each other's burdens, sometimes that includes sharing the grace received as we dealt with our own burdens. We can give others compassion because we've experienced similar pain and trials in our own lives.

I find it really sad when I hear of a woman who can't or won't share about her divorce with a newly divorced woman. It makes me wonder if she forgot that grace covered that divorce and God might want use her healing to help encourage others. But grace is there too as we all decide how much we share about our own lives with others, so we can share in their burdens.

2

Find Your Worth

You made all the delicate, inner parts of my body and knit me together in my mother's womb. Thank you for making me so wonderfully complex! Your workmanship is marvelous—how well I know it. You watched me as I was being formed in utter seclusion, as I was woven together in the dark of the womb. You saw me before I was born. Every day of my life was recorded in your book. Every moment was laid out before a single day had passed. How precious are your thoughts about me, O God. They cannot be

*numbered! I can't even count them; they
outnumber the grains of sand!*

—Psalms 139:13–8

IT WAS AN EARLY afternoon on an April Saturday when I finally got up the nerve to set a boundary and say to my (now ex-) husband to either go and buy groceries for our home or move out. I gave him the choice and I was okay with whatever he chose. He had already filed for divorce, and a judge had told him to keep providing for his family, but he'd refused. We were still living together and the bills hadn't changed. The only change was a third party he needed to impress.

Add to that, I had just spent my entire morning dragging my kids to a traveling food bank, where we stood outside for hours in the coldness of early spring with hundreds of other people. Without access to my own checking account, this was the only way I knew to make sure my kids were fed.

That day he chose to leave our home. Impressing someone else was more important than taking care of his family. This wasn't the first time he'd made that same choice, and as much as the sting wasn't as bad this third time, my heart nor my brain could comprehend why leaving would ever be a choice. But that's the choice he made, and this time I wasn't going to beg him to come back. I was done enabling him and was ready to start finding my worth in anything other than him. I had felt for too long that if my husband was able to reject me in such a cruel way, multiple times, I was just that unlovable. I was tired of feeling worthless and unaccepted.

Where We Find Worth

I had worn the titles of "wife" and "married" like badges of worthiness for myself, even through his multiple affairs. The titles made me feel important and loved. They had become what I thought would be my permanent identity. At the time, I believed I was created just for that purpose. I was defined by what I could do for those in my household, but I lived with no further purpose. My life revolved around them. While married, I would often feel bad for even breathing, not understanding that my maker, who saw me as His masterpiece, had loved me since before I even started breathing.

*For we are God's masterpiece, He has
created us anew in Christ Jesus, so we can
do the good things he planned for us long
ago.*

—Ephesians 2:10

We are loved, period. We are not loved for
what we can be for others. We are not worthy
based on how perfectly we perform, how pretty
we look, or how skinny we are, and especially
not for what we can do for others. We are loved
because God says He loves us.

Jesus was a part of the master plan to show
us love from our heavenly Father. He came to
earth so we could experience His great love and
healing. Jesus healed the sick. And then He took
the blame for all that man had done and had yet
to do. Why? Because it was all part of God's
rescue plan from the very beginning. Jesus
became the reason we are worthy just by being
alive. He made us worthy. What a wonderful gift
of love from God!

Your identity in Christ is so much more
important than any earthly identity, title, or what
others think about you. God knows your heart;
He created it. He wants to take all the broken
pieces of your heart, put them back together, and

use it all for His purpose.

But first He has to change your identity from unworthy to worthy, from unaccepted to acceptable in His sight, just like He did for me. The one who knows you inside and out sees you and calls you worthy.

Creating Something Beautiful

Imagine yourself as a living house. God comes in to rebuild that house. At first, perhaps, you can understand what He is doing. He is getting the drains right and stopping the leaks in the roof and so on: you knew that those jobs needed doing and so you are not surprised. But presently He starts knocking the house about in a way that hurts abominably and does not seem to make sense. What on earth is He up to? The explanation is that He is building quite a different house from the one you thought of—throwing out a new wing here, putting on an extra floor there, running up towers, making courtyards. You thought you were going to be made into a decent little cottage: but He is building a palace. He intends to come and live in it Himself.

—C.S. Lewis, *Mere Christianity*

Several years into my marriage, we bought a house that only needed some minor repairs ... or so we thought. On the outside, things looked great. The previous owners had done a lot of cosmetic updates. But hidden behind the freshly painted wooden paneling and stucco walls was untouched knob and tube electrical wiring that was one hundred years old. Then, when we started updating the upstairs bathroom floor, we found plumbing issues that we had to repair. The list goes on. Seven years to the day, we sold that house and moved into a rental. We weren't interested in investing any more time and energy into that mess. I just couldn't invest any more into a house I wasn't in love with. It wasn't worthy. Thankfully God doesn't see us the same way as I saw that house. He sees past our mess to what He wants to create.

Your heavenly Father's character is unlike any earthly being's. A human could ignore the fact that the house (you) needs a total gut job and major overhaul. But God never could. His great love and compassion for you makes sure you have all that is needed after a storm—like divorce. He doesn't just paint a few walls and patch a few broken pieces. He wants to bring your little house up to code and way beyond code by healing you, restoring you, and putting you on a firm foundation.

> *In his kindness God called you to share in his eternal glory by means of Christ Jesus. So after you have suffered a little while, he will restore, support, and strengthen you, and he will place you on a firm foundation.*

—1 Peter 5:10

I'm sure you're aware that God is quite the artist. He paints a breathtaking sunset every single night all over the world. And like a grandmother who takes the scraps from our old clothes or t-shirts to create a beautiful quilt, God wants to take every piece of your life, including all the pain and bruised places, and create a masterpiece. You may feel that He has already gutted your house. I know I felt that way too.

But God wants to dig even deeper, behind your cosmetic façade. He wants to remove your walls (the authentic you that you keep hidden inside), clean out all the shame from your past, and make you into the most beautiful version of you, with worth deeply rooted in God and His love for you.

He is making you into a masterpiece and He plans to live there. You just have to let Him in the door with His toolkit to do His handiwork.

I promise He can be trusted to get the job done, in His time, and with a master craftsman's touch.

You Are Loved

> *This is real love—not that we loved God, but that he loved us and sent his Son as a sacrifice to take away our sins.*

— 1 John 4:10

During my lowest points, I understood "God loves you," but I didn't feel that in my heart. My heart was filled with words said to me and about me, throughout my entire life, which sought to tear me down. The words left scars that turned into voices that told me I wasn't worthy. They were words I believed about myself.

One night during the divorce process, after a day dealing with the lawyers and my ex, I had had enough of everything I was going through. Court hearings weren't going the way I'd expected, or even the way I was told things would go.

I was trying to pay the bills but there was never enough, and I had no one to help me. I was trying to take care of the kids but I could barely take care of myself. I was plain worn out; and honestly, I was very angry with God and what I thought was His inaction at answering my prayers.

Thankfully we lived way out in the country, because one sleepless night at about 3:00 a.m., I screamed at the top of my lungs that I wasn't going to speak to Him again. He had left me alone on earth! I was done! So done! No longer a Christian, DONE! And you'd better believe I meant every word of it too. If this was what being a Christian meant, I no longer wanted any part of it. Life is hard after a divorce, and I wanted the easy life I thought I deserved. I wasn't the one sinning. I didn't deserve to feel like I was being punished for someone else's actions.

Next thing that happened, with ugly tears streaming down my face and rage in my heart, the Holy Spirit started praying on my behalf. I tried to stop it, because I didn't want to participate. I said I wasn't going to pray. I tried to fight it, but I was praying in my heart and I heard it in my head. If I hadn't been upset, I might have laughed.

Just then I started feeling a lot of love and compassion I had never felt before. I had been a confessing Christian for over fifteen years, but it was in that moment that I finally felt I was loved and accepted. It felt as if my daddy was looking down on me, chuckling, saying, "I know you didn't mean that! I still love you so much, my child."

Let me tell you, my sister, God looks at you the very same way. That's our Papa! And He sees all you've been through, He sees all that you face, He knows the stress and the struggles, and He still loves you just the same as He did during those days you spent in your mother's womb. He looks down on you in love.

See Yourself through God's Eyes

> *For you are all children of God through faith in Christ Jesus. And all who have been united with Christ in baptism have put on Christ, like putting on new clothes. There is no longer Jew or Gentile, slave or free, male and female. For you are all one in Christ Jesus.*

—Galatians 3:26–28

God doesn't see our outward appearances. He doesn't see the flaws we see in the mirror when we get out of bed every morning. He doesn't see how we've put on a few pounds or how we have a few wrinkles. He sees to the heart and the character of every person. He only sees our inner beauty, where we've grown, and our future. He no longer sees our sin because of the blood of Jesus. God sees righteousness through Jesus, who introduces us as His beloved daughters.

We are His bride. We are precious in His sight, and clothed in pure white garments.

When I was angry with God and told Him I never was going to believe in Him again, He saw past it all to my heart. He knew that I was really always for Him. He knew my rant was only my hurt, frustration, and anger over my circumstances. Even in my anger, He still accepted me. He can handle our wounded emotions and still give us love. In those moments, His love broke through to my jaded heart, to those inner spaces which needed love and compassion, just like the woman spoken about in Mark 5. I knew then my faith would allow God to heal me. That healing power broke through and started showing me just how He saw me. He spoke to my heart and said just what I needed to hear.

I had to stop looking at myself through my shame about my divorce, through my past mistakes, and through my imperfections. That was the voice I heard every time there seemed to be a setback. That voice was not one of love but the voice of my enemy, filling my mind with lies that no longer defined me. I learned that I was God's beloved.

God looks on you with love, with much care, and all the kindness in the world. He sees you as the finished product you will become: a masterpiece. Through His eyes you are loved. God has always loved you and He'll never stop. He accepts you through grace because of Jesus Christ. If God loves you, you are worth loving and being loved.

Personally, I've always had an easier time saying this than believing it, but I knew I had to give myself grace that healing is usually one step forward and two steps back. Loving myself and seeing myself as He saw me would be no different.

Remind Yourself You Belong to God

*And now that you belong to Christ, you
are the true children of Abraham. You are
his heirs, and God's promise to Abraham
belongs to you.*

—Galatians 3:29

What would you do if your child came to
you and said she was "fat, ugly, and worthless!"
after she was ditched by a friend at school? You'd
probably tell her those things were not true and
that she should never talk about herself in such
degrading ways. Friend or no friend, she is still
loved. Then the next morning, you look at
yourself in the mirror and say the very same
things about yourself, even if you don't speak the
words out loud. How is that any different from
allowing your daughter to speak to herself in
such ways?

When I changed the dialogue in my own
head and controlled what came out of my mouth
about myself to align it with truth, I started
believing it. It took time, but I was determined to
find my misplaced worth and to start loving
myself again. During my divorce healing,

I actually searched out faith-filled bloggers

and prophetesses who were speaking from the identity I wanted for myself. They used words like "redeemed," "His beloved," and "daughter of a King." Like them, I wanted to think those things about myself, but I had to hear them and accept them before I could believe them in my heart.

You are the daughter of a King.

Those are the words I had to keep speaking to myself to remind myself I belonged to my Father. Each time I said it, I believed it a little bit more. I had spent my entire life seeking validation from others, but my worth was never found in people. I found it in the value God gave me. It is not conceited to claim our identity and worth in this world, but for some reason, most of us don't. Speak value, worth, and love to yourself because of God's unconditional love for you. Praise God for how He has made you perfect in His sight. Don't allow the world to tear you down by focusing on what you are not. Instead, allow God's Word to speak to your heart and give you the worthiness you deserve as a child of the one true King.

Focus on the Cross

We do this by keeping our eyes on Jesus, the champion who initiates and perfects our faith.

—Hebrews 12:2a

For months when I went to church, I would literally sit there and keep my eyes fixated on the cross on the wall. During those long drawn-out months of the divorce process, and then into my healing, each day provided me with another set of challenges to face. What about health insurance? Who will help us move? How will I pay the bills next month? Will I find a job?

Most days I felt rather seasick on this rocking sailboat called life. And I felt so alone trying to make these hard decisions on my own. Each day as the storm raged and as I kept looking at my circumstances, my hope seemed to fade and anxiousness began to rise. If I wanted to stay hope-filled and full of peace, I had to remember to keep my eyes on the cross, remind myself that my end was very secure, and remember this earth was not my home. In doing that, my heart was calmed.

We have a palace waiting for us in heaven!

And when we claim that as our truth, we start to believe it. Our current circumstances do not change the long-term outcome we are heading toward. The end is secure no matter what we face.

Learn to focus less on your circumstances and more on the power over everything. The cross took back the glorious, triumphant ending. God is still in control, even when things feel out of control. Our circumstances have no power over us when we focus on the cross and what it means to us.

We need to keep the end in mind. God has it all worked out. When we seek God, He gives us His peace and joy, thanks to the Holy Spirit. When we surrender, we build a strong foundation in the Lord that can weather any storm.

3

You Deserve Self-Care

*Don't you realize that your body is the
temple of the Holy Spirit, who lives in you
and was given to you by God? You do not
belong to yourself, for God bought you
with a high price. So you must honor God
with your body.*

—1 Corinthians 6:19–20

THE MONTH BEFORE my husband left, I was
diagnosed with Systemic Lupus Erythematous

(Lupus) after spending years struggling with feeling physically ill much of the time. I didn't even tell him because I knew he didn't care. He'd stopped caring about my medical issues long before he left. And I just kept trying to do it all, not sharing how I was really feeling or what was going on.

Self-care had never been in my vocabulary. I was told I was selfish for wanting to do things for myself. For most of my life, I felt I was expected to be the main caregiver for those in my immediate family. I had done a very good job too. But all the psychological abuse I had endured, plus the stress and feeling totally overwhelmed, had taken its toll on my body. Putting everyone else first was killing me from the inside out, and I knew I would die if I didn't start seeing myself as equally important as everyone else.

At that point I realized I had no other choice *but* to start taking care of myself, because honestly, there was no one else around to do it. Some of us have to learn to take care of ourselves in the most difficult season of life.

Don't Self-Medicate

> *Don't copy the behavior and customs of*
> *this world, but let God transform you into*
> *a new person by changing the way you*
> *think. Then you will learn to know God's*
> *will for you, which is good and pleasing*
> *and perfect.*

—Romans 12:2

If you're feeling like your life is in shambles, you are not alone. The season of divorce is like walking in a desert. It's dry and the heat is on your back most of the time. It seems lonely, and most of the things you're used to having are gone. Your life and the lives of your children have been turned upside-down. Who knows what end is up?

Life will keep moving forward and the people around you will keep doing their jobs, while you seem to be stuck in a dry wasteland. Most of the people in your life, especially those who've never been through a divorce, might actually expect you to be healed and over everything by the time you hit a certain milestone, like the day everything is finalized or one year later. It's not uncommon to feel pushed in your healing based on what others think should be your timeline.

And sometimes it seems easier to put on a mask and hide your feelings so as to not be a burden or to disappoint anyone. Sometimes it seems easier to please others rather than deal with your pain. You may want to numb the pain so you can just get through each day. But these things only stop the healing process, give you no lasting comfort, and actually make things worse for the long term. Just like getting your college education, there are no quick-fix ways through your divorce pain. You have to keep at it one day at a time, sometimes one hour at a time, growing and learning through each pain and each new experience, taking baby steps toward the prize of not only surviving after divorce, but maybe even thriving.

Along the way there will be people who try to give you advice on what you can do to feel better, or they'll do things like take you "out on the town" (drinking or shopping), or try to set you up with another man (to make you happy), or worse, they'll tell you to get over it because they just can't stand to see you hurting another day. They may mean well, but their advice should be somewhat ignored. During times of loneliness, many turn to drinking, taking mind-numbing drugs, joining dating websites, or doing anything in excess to cope, but this only puts the pain and the problems on the backburner for a short while. Those who don't want to work through the pain or the feelings just want to numb them down and pretend they don't exist.

It's like not casting a broken bone. The bone doesn't heal, or if it does, it often heals in the wrong place or in the wrong way. Ultimately the bone will need to be rebroken in order to set it straight. Your heart needs the same type of healing. You need to set it straight and then work through each step of the phases of the grief process and divorce recovery. Allow God to heal you and to put everything back the way it is supposed to be.

Do the work, walk through the pain, and you'll be better for it.

You need to care about yourself that much to do things the right way. Not going that way? Then turn around and start from the beginning. God allows for U-turns because He loves you that much.

Side note: Please understand I'm not talking about needed anti-depressants or anti-anxiety drugs prescribed and monitored by a doctor. When I say "drugs," I mean an excess of painkillers, alcohol, or other drugs—legal or not—taken to numb the pain rather than working on the healing.

Love Yourself

> *The second is equally important: "Love your neighbor as yourself." No other commandment is greater than these.*

—Mark 12:31

Jesus made His followers aware of the two major commandments we need to follow: Love God and then love others. He also added, "as yourself." We cannot love anyone or even God if we don't love ourselves. We learn to love others after we learn to love ourselves. It's not selfish to focus on ourselves while we heal; that's really love, because it allows us to take care of the body God gave us so that we are better able to love others. Furthermore, our self-love allows us to be a temple for the Holy Spirit. When we love the temple God lives in, we also demonstrate that we love God because His Spirit lives inside us. Don't be in bondage to self-hatred; learn self-care instead.

You Need to Put Yourself First

I find it easy to get caught up in "doing" for others. I love writing, speaking, and the ministry God has anointed me for. I love caring for my children, sometimes too much. I've had a hard time saying no for fear of missing an opportunity to serve others or letting them down. God had to teach me that putting myself first was more important than any service I could do for others. I couldn't continue to love others while putting myself last. I was giving more than I had to give.

We do things for others out of the overflow of our own resources. When we give all of our resources away, leaving ourselves with nothing, we are depleted. That's when we start to feel angry, resentful, and frustrated toward the people we're trying to help. For people like me, our bodies point out that we've been giving way too much for way too long.

You would not forget to get your vehicle's oil changed for an entire year, yet expect your vehicle to keep going for you. Your body works in a similar way. Taking care of yourself is like maintenance for your body. Taking care of your body and doing things that make you feel rested fuels you. Without it, you will have nothing to give others and you'll burn yourself out. You're going to need all the strength you can get to raise children by yourself. I'm sure by now you're aware that there is no relay handoff person to take over when you've had enough. And single moms don't get sick days, so keeping yourself healthy is very important to the survival of your family.

Putting the effort into your self-care is going to take some intentionality and planning. You'll have to schedule time for yourself and/or take the time for yourself in small chunks whenever you can. Rest, relax, and recharge when the kids are gone on visitation, if possible. Also, give the kids a quiet time each day, or give them a set bedtime before yours so you have some time to yourself at night, or get up early in the morning. Fight for and make the time—whatever works for you. You are worth it; your family is worth it.

Manage Your Stress

> *God blesses those who work for peace, for they will be called the children of God.*

> —Matthew 5:9

We all manage stress using methods we were

taught by the generations before us. As adults, we have to make a choice to do things the way we were taught or decide on something better for us, preferably something a lot healthier than before. Divorce healing is the perfect time to look deep into your past and examine the patterns you've copied.

You can make the choice to create something different and healthier, not just for you, but also for your children to take into adulthood.

Divorce is usually a very stressful time. Tensions are high and there are lots of pressing circumstances outside your control. If you were married to a toxic or abusive husband, I'm sure I don't have to tell you that the stress level can go through the roof whenever the other person makes an already stressful situation much worse.

> *Never pay back evil with more evil. Do things in such a way that everyone can see you are honorable. Do all that you can to live in peace with everyone.*

> —Romans 12:17–18

In order to stay calm and keep the peace, remind yourself that you can only control yourself. How another person acts, even a husband or a child, does not reflect on you but on him. You'll feel so much better walking away with integrity if you don't participate in any dysfunction. Manage your stress by allowing God to protect you while you stay calm. "I am leaving you with a gift—peace of mind and heart. And the peace I give is a gift the world cannot give. So don't be troubled or afraid" (John 14:27).

I have found the best way to deal with a toxic person is to not respond in any other way than with a very monotone voice and a businesslike manner. Being assertive can help you feel good about how you are speaking, even if the other person is enraged. He hates it at first, but then he starts to realize that you're no fun to play with and he moves to someone else. The better you handle your stress or upset, the better you'll be at handling your ex-husband and your children in the future.

Some other healthy ways to handle stress are to make sure you get in that time with God. Remember, that's part of your healing to establish. Keep that close relationship with God. He can give you the strength to make it through this as calmly as possible while being the peacemaker.

As you begin to heal and grow, things will get much easier to handle.

Get Educated

> *Wisdom will save you from evil people,*
> *from those whose words are twisted.*
>
> —Proverbs 2:12

One of the key components to your self-care and a part of your healing is education. Education will unlock the wisdom you need to process what has happened to you, why you've made certain choices in your life, and how you should proceed and protect yourself in the future.

Education will teach you about childhood scars, emotional and psychological abuse, boundaries, healthy and unhealthy relationships—the good, the bad, and the evil— and so much more. This education helps you self-coach yourself to make the wisest choices in the future. Those who stick their head in the sand, refusing to gain wisdom from their experiences, tend to repeat the same mistakes over and over again until they learn. It's like going around the same mountain and not knowing how to get off it. You can keep making the same mistakes or learn a better, healthier way. The choice is always yours, but getting healthy the first time around is the quickest route to healing.

My favorite way to learn is to read books. I spend many a sleepless night reading to learn all that I can. Reading books is not the only way to learn. You can read blogs, watch YouTube videos, listen to podcasts, or join communities or groups on Facebook. You can look for social media pages that share information about Christian divorce, abuse healing, or whatever else you need to learn about.

There are lots of experts out there, but just remember Jesus is the only true healer—without Him, you cannot fully heal. In the back is a link to a list of resources that can help you in divorce recovery, abuse recovery, surviving after divorce, and more.

Close in Your Inner Circle

So follow the steps of the good, and stay on the paths of the righteous.

—Proverbs 2:20

Another aspect of divorce healing that I had to work through was learning to develop and seek out healthy relationships. When I was going through my divorce, I easily found, and unknowingly trusted, people who were just watching to see me emotionally bleed. They didn't really care about my situation, but they acted as if they did to hear all of the juicy details. Most people love to stand and watch as emergency workers clean up after an accident. I know this because I was one of those emergency medical workers as a young adult. People would drive really slowly past the crashed-up cars, hoping to catch a glimpse of something gory. People love a good train wreck. Don't provide it. Learn who is really on your side and who is just watching the destruction of your marriage and all that comes with it.

Learn from my mistake, close in your inner circle to only include loyal, trustworthy friends who have been by you for a very long time. Only allow your most supportive friends to know the details as they pray for you. If others want to know, just tell them to pray for you and leave it at that. God knows the details, so He doesn't need more than your name when they pray.

Sadly, I lost faith in a lot of people I thought I

could trust during my divorce. Once I was along in my healing and able, I had to separate from a lot more dysfunction than I would have if I had just closed in my inner circle from the beginning.

Find Ripe Fruit

> *When you produce much fruit, you are my true disciples. This brings great glory to my Father.*
>
> —John 15:8

I've always had a natural green thumb, but when I added a few succulents and a few other exotic plants to my home, I wasn't sure what I doing, so I visited my local library to find a book or two. Right away I found one book that was full of wisdom about caring for plants, which I found quite interesting. Did you know that in order to get your bromeliad plant to bloom, you can put it into a sealed plastic environment with a few ripe apples or a ripening banana? A closed-in circle of ripe fruit helps this plant to bloom. I believe we can use this same advice with our own growth.

To obtain personal emotional growth, we must surround ourselves with those who are healthy, or at least working toward getting emotionally healthy. Just like bad characters corrupt good character, rotten fruit will only ruin the rest of the fruit trying to bloom. We can either all ripen and bloom together, or we all rot.

During your divorce healing, it is a good idea to close in your circle of friends to a very small, select few to help you grow in your own emotional health, help keep you encouraged, and hold you up when you really need it. You gain more insight into what makes a healthy relationship, and you are given time to have only positive relationships in your new, improved life.

Even Moses had two supportive friends who held up his arms when he grew tired and could no longer hold himself steady (Exodus 17:11–12). We need those types of prayer partners willing to take the time to pray with us and for us, those willing to stand with us and hold space for us when we are too tired or weak.

What steps can you take to secure a loving support system with ripe fruits of the Spirit? Who do you know who is thriving after divorce that you might ask to be your mentor while guiding you through this dry desert we call divorce?

Boundaries Are Protection

I'm finding that when most people hear the word "boundaries," they think of a huge wall put up in anger to keep people out. Yes, I believe you should close in your inner circle and only talk about divorce issues with those you can really trust, but boundaries are only walls when they need to be. The rest of the time they are helpful tools, giving you a way of speaking assertively that allows you to keep yourself safe from future hurt or mistreatment.

Boundaries aren' t a way to control others, nor are they manipulative tactics.

They are limits we place on ourselves to keep the peace inside our own lives and our own homes. They dictate what we will and will not allow, like fences with gates keeping the good in and the bad out.

God created boundaries in the garden. He gave Adam and Eve just one major boundary and then consequences, which included leaving the garden, when they didn't respect God's boundaries (Genesis 3:23).

Joseph is another such biblical example of

healthy boundaries on display. After he was reunited with his brothers, he didn't allow them to hurt him again. Judah was the brother who had initiated the plan to get rid of Joseph (Genesis 37:26), so Joseph needed to test his heart for true repentance (Genesis 42:13). Joseph learned that Judah was willing to lay down his life for their youngest brother, Benjamin, which showed Joseph there was a clear change in his heart attitude. This showed repentance for the way he'd treated Joseph, whom the brothers thought had died because of their actions.

If Joseph, Adam, and Eve were clearly used by God and written about in His Word, then we should follow these examples and utilize boundaries as well. All healthy, loving relationships need boundaries. It's how we keep everyone safe and healthy. Those who respect our boundaries are healthy people to have in our lives, and in turn, we can and should respect their boundaries as well. This creates an environment for growth, and will contribute toward your self-care as you learn to not only survive after divorce, but to thrive.

Taking care of yourself is important. You are able to be the best version of yourself and live an intentional life full of peace, with a healthy body, heart, and soul that support you as you love God and love others.

4

Survival Strategies

She equips herself with strength [spiritual, mental, and physical fitness for her God-given task]. And makes her arms strong.

—Proverbs 31:17 AMP

WHILE YOU'RE DEALING with the trauma of divorce, it might be hard to think about how you're going to survive now, and especially once everything is settled. Life becomes more about who needs what right this second, with no energy left to do anything else.

According to the *Oxford English Dictionary,* survival is "the state or fact of continuing to live or exist, typically in spite of an accident, ordeal, or difficult circumstances." In the beginning there is no life, just survival: you're waking up, mindlessly blowing through the day while getting the bare minimum done, and then crashing into bed, to do it all over again the next day. I vividly remember those first days of mere survival. My brain hurt to think and I couldn't wait to get back into bed. Extreme exhaustion and pain from the grief was controlling my life. I was hoping it was a nightmare I'd soon wake up from. But I never woke up. I had to learn to get past that phase.

I know you're probably struggling just like I did. Or you're overwhelmed with all the duties of being the only parent. Trust me, as hard as this is going to sound, now is the best time to get your household in order—before the kids get used to pushing over Mom and manipulating the situation. Even in this chaos of divorce, their underdeveloped brains are still learning. They notice that you're just too exhausted to do anything about their behavior or lack of cooperation, so of course they'll try to take advantage.

> *My help comes from the Lord, who made heaven and earth!*

—Psalm 121:2

It's time to embrace this life. It's time to pull from God's strength within you and put one foot in front of the other. Be consistent and intentional in how you're working through the issues and reclaiming your home and your family. I don't know why divorce happens, but it does. Embracing it means stepping into the unknown future with a known God and trusting that He will be with you the entire way. It's *not* about being perfect. It's *not* about putting your feelings aside or pretending life is fine. It's just about making progress each day toward the goals of healing your life and your home, while giving yourself grace as you move from merely surviving to enduring, and then to thriving. Each time you feel weak, remember God is your strength and you *can* endure this season. Call on your friends and prayer warriors to hold up your arms in prayer, as you build the muscles in your own arms to carry you through.

Be Present

For when I am weak, then I am strong.

—2 Corinthians 12:11

During this time it will be so easy to try to escape everyday parenting. Easy to check out of problems and issues not related to the divorce, easy to pretend they don't exist. Everything is pressing and everyone needs you, while you just want to crumble in a mess on the floor. Decisions need to be made, appointments must be attended, and for some reason, lenders and utility companies still want their money every month.

As you're feeling your pain and feeling overwhelmed, so are your children. They are needy because they feel the loss, and they more than likely blame themselves for all that is going on. They don't understand that these are adult problems and that children are never the cause of divorce. Divorce also forces your family to make huge changes. Most of those changes affect the kids too. They need to look up to someone who will take the lead into this foreign territory, who will comfort and reassure them that everything is going to be okay. You can be their guide, even if you are only a few steps ahead of them. Allow

God to guide you as you step up to lead the whole house into healing.

Take Your House Back

> *But as for me and my family, we will serve the Lord.*

> —Joshua 24:15

The most important thing you need to remember right now is: you are *still* a family! One missing parent doesn't make you broken (damaged beyond repair). Living in an abusive or adulterous marriage is broken. You could never live a healthy life with someone who dumps his toxic waste (or commits adultery or has addiction problems he refuses to deal with) on you daily. Divorce is fixable. God is the perfect healer.

Today or tomorrow is the best day to reclaim your family and free it from the grips of this destruction. See yourself, and conduct your household, as a family unit from this moment on. God is with you and goes before you.

> *Do not be afraid or discouraged, for the Lord will personally go ahead of you.*

> *He will be with you; he will neither fail*

you nor abandon you.

—Deuteronomy 31:8

If you sat down to dinner together as a family most nights, then continue doing so. Continue to read your Bibles together and find times to worship together. If what you did before is too stressful, then find a new, different way to continue with the same routines. New experiences can replace the old memories as you grow through this together.

Call a family meeting and set up the ground rules of the house. Let the kids help you decide on the consequences for breaking the family rules. Although they might fight these rules, setting them up now will bring some normalcy, routine, and stability to their lives.

They'll thank you someday. Just probably not today. God is still the Lord of your house and of your family. You have to trust Him to guide you as the new leader and teacher of the home. Ask for His assistance and He will guide your paths.

Create Routine

Commit your actions to the Lord, and

your plans will succeed.

—Proverbs 16:3

I know people, like myself, who love routine, and I know even more people who run by the seat of their pants. I was married to the latter. Because of this, we lived for years with lack of peace and any feelings of normalcy in our home. No one knew what each day would bring or what the schedule was. One day the kids would get in trouble for the very thing they had done the week before without issue. There was a lot of noise, yelling, frustration, and chaos until the day he left. That day I was finally free to run the house in the way I saw fit. I think we all breathed a sigh of relief when he moved out. We felt peace

Take back your home.

To take back my home, the very next day, we sat at the breakfast table and had a family meeting. It was time to set up a daily schedule for us, a schedule that gave the kids and myself a flexible routine to follow. I knew this would be the best way to get us through the upcoming divorce and all the chaos that would come with that. Having a semi-set routine gives children comfort: they know what they can expect and where their limits are. Not only that, I was better able to handle my own stress because having a daily routine, having house rules, having boundaries, and feeling like a team helped our house to be more peaceful.

Get Everyone to Contribute

> *Even while we were with you, we gave you this command: "Those unwilling to work will not get to eat."*
>
> —2 Thessalonians 3:10

Children of all ages can contribute to their family by helping out around the house.

You, Mom, can' t be expected to do it all.

Any good team picks up the slack when others are down or players are out. The same goes for your family. Each should contribute with age-appropriate responsibilities and contributions so you can all work together as a family unit. This not only teaches them how to clean and shows each other support, it also gives them a sense of accomplishment. After the routine is in place, you'll realize that you are running the house like a well-oiled machine. Not perfectly, but it's still progress when all the family members know their individual expectations, even if they forget almost every day. This also frees you from some of the stress of home care and makes you better able to be present in your kids' lives.

Honestly, it can be enjoyable to be around them as well. We all know that kids need stability during difficult times, but they also need to have bouts of your undivided attention. They need reassurance, some more than others. They need to know that you love them, you're there for them, and you will never leave them. Show them you're always there for them. Make time for them. And help them to find the healing they need as well.

Creating a family routine will free you up to deal with the adult issues while the kids fight over whose turn it is to unload the dishwasher. We don't eat until someone gets it done, even if we have to contribute to get it done, as a team.

Create a Budget

But don't begin until you count the cost. For who would begin construction of a

*building without first calculating the cost
to see if there is enough money to finish
it?*

—Luke 14:28

Creating and keeping a budget is an important tool for any divorced woman or single mother. Unless you have an abundance of financial resources, your cash is going to be limited. You've become the sole provider, even if you do receive child support. It might be easy to just shop away your stress, or make up for the loss of your husband with toys or fun days out with Mom, but this could leave you in a financial crisis very quickly. Knowing how much money you need to survive and how much money you have for nonessentials is important, and will keep things secure for you and your kids.

In my opinion, and according to Dave Ramsey of Financial Peace University, the first necessity should be to secure an emergency fund—so you don't have to rely on others to bail you out in an emergency—if you don't have one already. Emergencies happen to all families, and not having a husband to rely on can cause excess stress that you don't need right now. An emergency fund is for just that, emergencies. The minimum amount I suggest would be two rent or house payments or $1,000, whichever is higher. This way, if you lose a job or child support just stops, and it could, you have two months to get things back on track.

Also, while you're setting up your emergency fund, you need to list out all your income and expenses numbers to make sure they match up. Create a written household budget. If things don't match, now is the time to fix that. Get rid of any unnecessary expenses and luxuries. If you can, create a monthly entertainment budget and share with the kids how much is in it for things you used to do but have to limit now. If they are older, ask them if they prefer to get rid of cable TV or weekly pizza night. If you can't afford either, that's fine too. This helps them to understand that we all have to make sacrifices to separate the family into two different households.

We all have to make sacrifices.

They may not like it, but it's better that they face the truth now, rather than later.

Seek out government assistance if you know you can't afford to cover groceries, medical insurance, or other essentials to survive. There is no shame is seeking help; that's what these resources are for. It's a part of life, and many of us need it during hard times.

My son does a terrific job at trying to bribe me into getting way too many treats while at the store. We didn't always have the money. Trusting God to provide, I started using coupons again, which I had done during the times my former husband was unemployed. There are resources out there to help you. Look for ways to bring in more income, sell things you no longer use, and change things up to save or earn more money each month.

And yes, Dad might play the game that he can and will do everything for them, but you don't have to compete.

You don' t have to compete.

Stand your ground and defend the budget as being what it is. Because my son was experiencing a Disney-like time when visiting his dad, he thought he could ask the same of me. Instead, I let it be known that I would not be buying love, nor would I replace the guilty feelings with presents.

Showing my child the income and expenses sheet, and explaining how they often didn't match up every month, helped him to realize why I said no most of the time. Once he was old enough to understand, there was less expectation to compete with the same type of lifestyle. Now my child understands that it's the budget that makes that decision, and it's not that he has a mean mom.

Find Your Community

Share each other's burdens, and in this way obey the law of Christ.

—Galatians 6:2

Personally, the loss of my marriage also meant the loss of family support. Both of my parents had passed away while I was married, and I had spent all my married years devoting my time and energy to taking care of my husband. We'd moved away from support systems, so I was literally left abandoned during a season of isolation and psychological abuse. I had only a small list of local friends, but no community or church support. All I could do was pray for God to show me where my community was.

I found three sets of communities to help me during this time. Since we were members of a homeschool community, they were the ones I reached out to first to help me with my children. Even right now, as I write this, my teenage son was picked up by another local mom to go to an activity. This allows me quiet time to write and get other work done. But the only way I get the help is if I ask for it.

I have to ignore my pride and release the feelings triggered when asking for help, and remind myself that I'm asking because I do really need the help. I would ask someone to watch my child while I went to "an appointment," but I didn't have to share that the appointment meant court or whatever else I was doing. Finding your community doesn't mean you have to reinvent your small inner circle or share personal information with people you may not trust.

The other community I found helpful was the local Divorce Care support group community. That group of ladies knew exactly what I was going through. I was safe to share my struggles and ask for prayers for court, and I felt less alone in this journey. They shared that what I was feeling was very normal and I was moving along in my healing, just like they had. Their support and example showed me there was hope ahead for me, as long as I was working on and seeking God for my healing.

I also joined a church small group that included couples and singles, both older and younger than myself. I had to step outside my comfort zone to find communities in my area. I had to walk up to people and introduce myself, something I had never really done before. Growing up, my mother would tell me to never invite myself, but I had to ask to join gatherings or to bring dinner to another single woman's house, with a board game, to get to know her. I even found a rental house with a fire pit, and together we learned how to start and manage a fire. I then invited parts of my community over to have what we called bond-fires: we'd bond over burned marshmallows and warm cookies. As scary as it was at the time, those people are some of my closest friends now.

Through these very different communities, I found what I needed from each. I learned to not share too much, especially at first, as not everyone needs to, or even wants to, hear your story. I learned that some people want to help single mothers, they just don't know how until we ask; and when we ask them, they are excited to lend a hand. This has helped me to take back my home and to heal, so I can be present in my kids' lives. We also grew as a family and found the resources to survive and heal.

5

Help the Children

Father to the fatherless, defender of widows—this is God, whose dwelling is holy.

—Psalm 68:5

WE OFTEN HEAR that kids will bounce back after divorce with just a little time. We hear they will get used to the idea of the divorce or that they'll move on quickly once everything is final.

But some kids don't, and even the ones who seem to be okay are often just hiding their pain behind a mask so they don't burden anyone. They are dealing with internal chaos but don't feel they can share it with others. They often don't want to bother you because they see all that you're going through.

Even adult children hurt after the divorce of their parents. Not to add more stress to your life, but we need to help our children during *and* after divorce, even if they seem to be fine about it. Unfortunately too many try to skip this step, which leads to problems down the road. Given the fact that there are so many people with unsolved childhood trauma and emotional issues, I would err on the side of getting unnecessary help rather than nothing at all. Many adults are still hurting because of childhood memories of abandonment by one or more parents. Furthermore, it's much easier to help a child heal than repair a deeply wounded adult.

John T. Chriban, PhD, ThD, shares in his book, *Collateral Damage: Guiding and Protecting Your Child Through the Minefield of Divorce:*

> The results from the Divorce Study reveal one painful yet undeniable fact: whether a divorce is amicable or acrimonious, children

often feel alone, unheard, and rejected. The most striking finding of the Divorce Study is the dramatic disparity between the ways parents and their children assess the impact of divorce. Most parents do not recognize how disruptive divorce is for their children and do not respond to their children's needs.

My research leaves little doubt that unless parents address the challenges of divorce for their children, it will be a harmful turning point in their lives.

This is proof that we can do better for our children. I think we all know at least one adult whose parents divorced during his childhood and he was forced to figure out his healing journey alone while Mom was working, dating, or worse. Some are in therapy for that to this day, and even more need it but don't get the help they need.

I think if we help our children through this time, we can facilitate health for them as adults. This is very easy advice for me to give while I struggle to help my own children to heal, years after their parents' divorce. All children heal differently. Kids are not meant to experience the trauma of their parents' separation. I believe that's why God hates divorce: not because He loves the institution of marriage or because He thinks marriage is more important than people, but because He loves the people in these families and knows they will hurt after the marriage is torn in two.

God loves your children more than you do.

Sometimes kids don't know how to deal with their pain, and many take that pain with them everywhere they go—even into their own marriages, doing exactly what happened to them as children. They repeat the dysfunctional patterns without even realizing, trying to heal but never given the tools to do so. We can help try to stop the cycle of abuse and/or divorce by helping our children now. The final outcome for our children's future rests on their own shoulders, even if we want them to make different, better decisions. We can only do our best to be present and intentional parents, guide our children, and ask God for His will in each and every situation.

Let me add some hope and encouragement here. As of writing this book, I have children who are not following Christ. And as much as I feel guilt for their unresolved pain, I carry no shame or blame for their adult choices. I've handed the rest of their raising over to God, knowing He loves them way more than I ever could. He pursues every lost sheep and wants to heal all who seek Him.

Seek the Father

If you want to heal and grow as a family, and help your children to move on to be healthier adults, then you need to seek God to help you be the best parent you can be while working on your own emotional healing and growth. You might be their only example, so do the very best that you can.

> *For your Creator will be your husband;*
> *the Lord of Heaven's Armies is his name!*
> *He is your Redeemer, the Holy One of*
> *Israel, the God of all the earth.*
>
> —Isaiah 54:5

As hard as it is, do not pull the kids into the middle of everything. Tell them the truth, but don't use them to communicate with your ex-spouse. Don't put them in situations where they have to decide on their loyalty; don't pull them into the middle of your latest argument. They want to be loyal to you both, just like when you were a two-parent family. They need your permission to love, respect, and care about the other parent, even if he is a lousy parent.

You can't always control what your ex-partner says about you when the children are with him, but you can control how you speak about your ex, and you can choose to participate in the dysfunction or not.

Personally, I choose to disengage from all of those situations, even if my children are constantly pulled into the middle. This gives me opportunities to teach boundaries while I use them myself in front of my child (the child still at home with me). As you work on your own healing, you can share that healing wisdom with your children. Give them examples of how other people are using boundaries well, or share experiences where using assertive speaking verses other options has helped you to have better relationships. This will take a lot of your energy, which is why self-care is so important, but in the end it will be well worth it.

Equally important is accepting God as your husband and the father of your children. There were many days when I called on my heavenly partner to help me parent my child. I felt so blessed when I saw Him assisting me in his raising. He wants to help us be the best single parents we can be. I believe God knew you would be doing this parenting thing alone. He knew you would need to depend on Him for support and strength.

He has equipped you for this job ahead.

He will fill in the gaps where only one parent can't be two.

I have found that God often answers my prayers for help and guidance even before I pray. Things have arrived at our doorstep before I even knew we would need it. His constant provision has helped me to not doubt His promises, especially when He surprises me with an abundance of blessings. I believe God delights in sharing His love and proving it to us in surprising ways. He wants to care for you and for your children. He wants to be your caretaker, your provider, and your protector. He won't force it, but He waits for you to call to Him for assistance.

What to Expect during Divorce

Expect that your children may regress in their development. Bedwetting might surface or resurface, as well as thumb-sucking, carrying security objects, and more. There might be lots of crying, tantrums, or silence, depending on how each child responds. Expect they will act out their feelings in all the wrong ways. They may bully others or find the bullies in every part of their lives. Older kids may rebel for a time, refusing to deal with anything.

They'll go through all the stages of grief, much the same as an adult, but it will look a little different. They may beg for marriage restoration: most kids, no matter the circumstances surrounding the divorce, want to see both of their parents together. They may be angry and frustrated that they aren't getting their way. Some even blame the innocent parent for not doing more to fix everything, although they often feel the divorce was ultimately their fault for not being a good enough child for the parent who left.

Sometimes kids don't know how to deal with all of their feelings and carry the pain and hurt with them everywhere they go, yet hiding it from those who may criticize them for it, especially years later. Help them to name those feelings. That's where the program Divorce Care for Kids (DC4K) at our local church helped us. Attending a class helps to get your child around other kids who know how they feel. There are instruction times with lessons that include how to put words to their feelings. The group we attended gave us a feelings chart, that we hung in the kitchen, so we could name how we were feeling each day (or each hour, if needed). Don't have a DC4K near you? Then buy a feelings chart and other books recommended in the endnotes to help talk through everything they might be feeling. A licensed counselor might also have feelings therapy games he or she can play with your children to help them.

Create a Safe Haven

Turn away from evil and do good. Search for peace, and work to maintain it.

—1 Peter 3:11

I knew I wanted a very different home environment than the one I'd grown up in and the one we had when I was married, so once I left the marriage home, I decided that our new home was going to be a safe haven. I immediately put boundaries in place to leave all the dysfunction of others out, as well as products (movies, video games, etc.) or people (new "boyfriends" or unhealthy family members) that made healing more difficult. Children don't need added stress, so creating a safe haven allows them to have a calm place when anxiety tries to take over.

Personally, I have worked on myself enough to learn what my triggers are. When I feel triggered, I retreat to my bedroom and close the door. I feel very comfortable and safe in my bedroom. My son also feels safe in there, so if I'm not escaping from him, he may come in my bedroom to feel safe as well. And although it has taken years of nights of him sleeping on my floor, he has also learned this technique for himself: he feels safe if he retreats to his own room at times when he feels triggered, upset, or anxious.

During times when he gets out of control or brings home stress with him, I allow him to vent if he can control his anger at the same time. If things get out of control, a period of stress decompression is needed so the house still feels safe for everyone who lives here. Once he's calmed down, we talk about and then work through the issue together, creating an action plan or dealing with the feelings as we need to.

Your home should be your safe place, not just a place where you and your children store belongings or participate in daily activates, but more of a place that you all go to to be calmed or soothed, and find peace from unnecessary dysfunction and outside noise. It's also good to be your authentic self in your safe haven. Masks can be removed as you and your children work through the feelings during and after divorce. Hiding will only prolong the healing, so your home should be the place where you find freedom to just *be,* where you can deal with things as they come in in the most peaceful way that you are able to at the time.

You are the gatekeeper to your life and your home.

You get to decide who or what comes in and what needs to stay out. If it doesn't contribute to the peaceful home you are now trying to have, then it should stay out. That's how I now manage my home. That's how I've reclaimed my peace after divorce.

Be Honest with Them

Personally, I don't think it's ever okay to lie to a child. I think everything should be age appropriate of course, but honesty is always the best policy. I believe you can share the truth with your child, even about another parent, without disrespecting that person, sinning, or dragging your children into the middle. It takes practice to talk in a way that doesn't share details but tells the truth about a given situation, even someone's sin problem, but it can be done.

During and after a divorce, children experience loss of trust in both parents.

Their world has been shaken by divorce no matter the reason. What they expected to be the status quo of their intact family unit has become destruction. They will need to learn to build trust, no matter who is to blame. This is very normal.

> *Don't lie to each other, for you have
> stripped off your old sinful nature and all
> its wicked deeds.*
>
> —Colossians 3:9

Unless there is a written gag order preventing you from talking with your children, be that truth-teller in your children's lives, even if you're the only one telling the truth and even if they don't believe you. Those with integrity tell

the truth at all times, so let them witness
integrity through you. Don't offer them any false
hope for marriage reconciliation, because almost
every child wishes for his parents to reunite.
They come to accept it and are better able to heal
if you remind them that the marriage is over and
final. Support their need for discussion and give
answers to their questions. Teach them to always
tell the truth by doing the same yourself.

Lastly, no matter how they turn out, how
your ex behaves, or what decisions they choose
to make, truth will always win. You can't control
the circumstances but you can control yourself.
Keep working on your own healing; keep
learning to have healthy boundaries and healthy
relationships. They are watching.

Teach Them Differently

> *To discipline a child produces wisdom, but
> a mother is disgraced by an undisciplined
> child.*
>
> —Proverbs 29:15

As you're focusing on your children, also
look at what kinds of relationships they have.
Teach them to set boundaries with those who

might hurt them, even if it's their own father. We can't force them to do anything, but we can give them the tools to protect themselves.

It is so hard to see our children getting hurt. The first things we want to do are step in and protect them like the mama bear we often are. But sometimes God is teaching them a lesson, even at an early age. If we're forced to share children with someone who acts like a child much of the time, we must allow our children to step up to the plate and learn how to defend themselves. What if God has allowed this divorce for the betterment of your children? What if they'll learn how to have boundaries and be healthier people because of all they've been through? Think of the compassion for orphans and widows they'll have because they've experienced it firsthand.

One of the things I learned was that I could only control how I parented my children. I want my children to be respectful of others. In order to do that, I had to rise above the disrespect sent toward me and be respectful anyway. This is why, when it is time for my child to leave for visitation, we have created a habit of making sure things are completely ready to go several minutes beforehand. That way he's prepared and ready to walk out of the door as soon as the car pulls into the driveway.

Model healthy respect.

I can't control every situation, or a last-minute potty break, but the routine is to be ready at least five minutes before the scheduled time. Not only is this respectful, it teaches respect for other people's time. I also send him out the door with a reminder to be home on time, even though I can't control that either.

One day this child is going to get a job, and he or she is going to look to his or her parents to learn how to act toward the boss in charge. I can teach him respect by modeling it. But if I'm contributing to the disrespect just because my ex-husband is, this will be the only example this child has on how to behave with any authority figure.

Then Leave the Rest to God

> *Direct your children onto the right path, and when they are older, they will not leave it.*

> —Proverbs 22:6

At some point, all parents have to learn to let go of their children and trust God with the rest. Sadly, mothers with shared physical custody have to let go sooner. This is where trusting God as their eternal Father comes into practice. When we surrender our children to their other parent, we have to trust God that there is a purpose to all of this. After they leave our house, our control over parenting ends.

I leave the rest in God' s hands.

He will parent my child, whom He loves, when my child is not with me. I pray for my children's protection, but the end result is left up to God. I have to trust Him and His will in every situation.

You might not be the most popular parent, especially after divorce. But you *can* be the parent God wants you to be, the parent your kids need you to be: with boundaries, being present, and teaching them respect and an emotionally healthy way of living after divorce. Reduce as much of the impact on the kids as you can, as you work on yourself to create a peaceful life they can follow. They are watching and learning as you handle life's big challenges. Even if you're the only one, show them how to handle it like a

Christian adult who trusts God with the unseen, and sometimes uncertain, future.

6

Accepting the Path before You

No, dear brothers and sisters, I have not achieved it, but I focus on this one thing: Forgetting the past and looking forward to what lies ahead.

—Philippians 3:13

THE END OF MY MARRIAGE meant the end of fighting for something I believed in: my commitment to God to stay faithfully married until death, no matter the circumstances. It hurt to know I had spent all those years putting so much effort into something, into someone, to have nothing to show for it but a broken heart.

I had come to a place of acceptance that my marriage was over. It had been dead for a long time, but I kept trying to revive it and bring it back to life. Sadly I was doing so alone. I'm not sure I was ever even loved in that marriage, and waiting for someone else to put in as much effort as I was, was only hurting my soul.

Many times there had been an "out" for me and I dismissed it. Many times I was free from the oppression and I took it all back. I had to wonder if God had a better plan than marriage reconciliation for my life. It was like I had missed the exit on the highway and now God was saying it was time to set me straight.

I prayed and told God that if He didn't want my marriage to continue, I would not fight for it any longer. As much as it hurt me to stop fighting, I would pray for my husband's heart to change until the day the divorce was final, but after that I would learn to come to accept the divorce as being what was best for my children and myself. I surrendered my will to whatever God had willed for my marriage, divorce, and life ahead.

Because my ex-husband had already moved on to seeing other women while we were still married, and he showed no signs of repentance for any of his sinful acts, even lying to me and others about this, I realized this was likely the final end. I also knew I could not change him or his heart, so my best bet was to start working on how I would put the lives of my children and myself back in a stable place.

This helped me to focus on embracing this new chapter and figuring out how we'd survive. Taking care of my husband was no longer in my hands. The weight of that responsibility was *Yes* making me physically sick, and I was glad to lay it down at the cross and walk away. —*Yes*

That's exactly what I did, and I am so much better for it now. *I'm looking forward to feeling better*

Stuck in the Desert

Then the Lord said to Moses, "Why are you crying out to me?

Tell the people to get moving!

—Exodus 14:15

As I mentioned before, going through a divorce can feel like you are walking in the dry sands of the desert. As I read the stories of the Israelites in the desert, I can really understand their struggle and their initial celebration about going from what they had known to the unknown (Exodus 15). Their celebration quickly ended, and mistrust for God's provision started to make them weary and lack faith. What should have been an eleven-day journey turned into forty years. That's because they could not embrace the change that leaving the oppression in Egypt meant for them. It was hard, no doubt, just like divorce. The years since my divorce have included many unknowns and days of struggle. I still may not fully know what the future holds for my children or me. But I do know who holds our future.

The Israelites became very weary during those years of depending on God for everything, and their old habits started to surface many times. God wanted them to let go of their old lives and to become totally dependent and obedient to only Him, but they often fell away from following these essential foundations. Much like us today, they were creatures of habit and found it easier to worship the seen than honor the unseen and give the glory to God. They only chose to focus on their circumstances instead of on God, who was clearly right there with them.

I have seen many people fall into this same trap. We cannot see God so we assume He is not there for us, even when He sends us proof. We want clear guidance with an easy road, but we have a hard time waiting on God or accepting His ways. God wants us to surrender to His will and walk forward, even if it means blindly trusting Him the entire time for everything. He wants us to keep moving forward while trusting that He has got our backs and won't let us fail. He tells us that He goes before us, but we forget that He's already there. This seems hard for many to do, even myself at times.

I heard a pastor once say (paraphrasing), "God closed the Red Sea not only to save the Israelites from the Egyptians who were chasing them, but also so that they had no passage back to their oppressors." God knew they would think it easier to go back. Many separated or divorced women feel that as well because of guilt and shame. They get stuck in the desert because they're unable to see God's plan or purpose, even for their divorce. The Israelites were fighting the process that God had to take them through to prepare them for the Promised Land. They grumbled and turned their backs on God each time things were hard or difficult. But what they didn't realize was that if they'd just let go of their need to control the situation and surrendered to God's will, things would have moved along a lot quicker.

He needs to take you through that same process—from oppressed slave to holy child of God. You need to embrace the change and your new life ahead.

What Is God's Will for Your Marriage?

> *"He is your Redeemer, the Holy One of Israel, the God of all the earth. For the Lord has called you back from your grief—as though you were a young wife abandoned by her husband," says your God.*

—Isaiah 54:5–6

Understand God's heart.

To understand the Word, we must understand God and His heart for the oppressed and those cast aside. In Malachi, we read that God hates divorce (2:16) because of the cruelty of divorce on the innocent party. During the time that was written, God was speaking to the priests who were allowing mixed marriages—between believers and unbelievers (Ezra 9:1)—which was causing men to divorce their Jewish wives, marry foreigners, and break their promise to keep God first in their lives.

I truly believe sometimes God releases women from marriage because He knows how much better life will be for them after the divorce is final. I believe He allows for divorce when the marriage is emotionally or physically killing an innocent party, or when the husband is coming between a woman and God. I believe there should be no judgment on the innocent party—defined as the non-adulterous, non-abusing, non-addicted, non-abandoning partner—even if he or she chose to leave or sought out a divorce.

The Lord loves all of His people and only wants what is best, so I believe for a lot of us, He took us back, just like He did the Israelites. He knew you could never grow or flourish as long as you were with a tyrant for a husband and/or being violated by adulterous acts. God's will is so much better than that marriage.

Has God closed that Red Sea door for you so that you can't go back into your toxic marriage? Is marriage reconciliation even an option? The answer is always no if there is a third party involved. Even if not, is that something God wants for you and your children? Is it something you want for yourself? These are important questions you need to ask yourself as you learn to embrace the future and survive after divorce.

Personally, I had to sit down and write out the pros and cons to help me come to an acceptance that going back was never an option. It wasn't really that I wanted to go back, but I was shackled with guilt and needed to be reminded of the truth. So one side of the paper had all the cons of my new divorced life and the other side of the paper was what married life was like.

For a time I pulled that paper out when I was thinking back to the good times and wondering if I had made a huge mistake. I was immediately reminded that God's will for my marriage was ... divorce.

God Wastes Nothing

And we know that God causes everything to work together for the good of those who love God and are called according to his purpose for them.

—Romans 8:28

God doesn't cause divorce, but He *does* take the broken pieces of our lives and stitch them back together into something beautiful. That beautiful house is where He will live and the Holy Spirit will guide. He also wants to make your life a living testament to His healing power, His daily provision, His amazing grace, and His acceptance for all divorced Christian women. There is a purpose for all of it.

When I read the Bible, I see story after story of lives filled with sin and destruction, but then God used everything for good and turned each one into a story of redemption. I often felt like my family had become just another statistic of abuse and divorce in America, but then He started showing me how I'd use my experiences to help guide others through their circumstances. I could write and share so others would know they were not alone. I was also invited to come speak at my local Divorce Care group—to share encouragement and my recovery story to help those in the early stages of their own divorce stories.

I'm the opposite sharing too much

I don't know what you could do, but don't let the shame of divorce keep you from sharing your story with someone, even if only in private. I've met too many people who keep it locked inside, saying it doesn't bother them, when they wear the scars of anger and bitterness on the outside.

Giving the past purpose is part of your healing.

It empowers you to not hold onto it like rotten fruit. Bring it all into the light. Lay it at the cross so you no longer carry any shame. No one is perfect and we all have our own issues. Divorce doesn't define who you are in Christ. And those who walk in the light will never walk in darkness again.

> *I am the light of the world. If you follow me, you won't have to walk in darkness, because you will have the light that leads to life.*
>
> —John 8:12

Just like the sun brings light into the world every morning, Jesus brings His light into the dark places of our hearts to outshine the darkness. God shines forth the light so we can see the way to our purpose. I believe God has written some wonderful, beautiful stories of marriages saved and restored through God's healing. Keep in mind that in those cases, both parties were willing to put in 100 percent of an effort to make those broken marriages work. And the spouses who needed serious help for their destructive ways of dealing with issues sought the help on their own to please God and not to impress man. Those stories are rare while stores of divorce are the norm.

God has written many more stories of women saved and lives restored and redeemed without the marriage, when divorce was the only option. One person cannot save a marriage. Many times after, those lives were used for a purpose. Beauty comes out of hurting, healing, and a complete reliance on God for every single need. He will use you too, if you let Him. He uses the redeemed to share the loving redemptive story of Jesus Christ.

I truly believe God has a purpose for every trial we face. A divorce trial might be the hardest thing you ever face, but I know that with the Lord's healing power, you will get through this time and come out with a much stronger faith on the other side. Accept the path before you and allow Him to use everything for good.

7

Moving On

*"For I know the plans I have for you," says
the Lord. "They are plans for good and not
for disaster, to give you a future and a
hope."*

—Jeremiah 29:11

MOST PEOPLE ASSOCIATE "moving on" to be
returning to the dating world and finding their
next spouse. Have you heard this before? "When

are you going to start moving on with your life?"
is often said way before you are ready to start
dating. The world has some sort of idea that the
only way for a divorced woman to be happy is if
she is dating and/or remarrying, like this is the
only way God can redeem and restore her life.
But I want to challenge that line of thinking and
redefine the phase "moving on" for Christians
after divorce.

I believe that you can and should move on
before you ever consider joining the dating world
again. I believe it's possible to be happy without
finding a man to fill the space your husband left. I
don't believe you need another half because you
are whole and complete by yourself, with God by
your side.

I have moved on with my life without dating
anyone. That's because I've worked through
much of my healing. I've come to terms with the
past. I've embraced this single life and all that it
has to offer. And I now do things like writing this
book and a blog to help others who are going
through a divorce. Who has time for dating when
you have so many wonderful things going on in
your life?

Also, I have learned from my mistakes,
accepted what is, and mourned what was lost.

I've returned to doing the things I used to love to do and picked up a few new hobbies along the way, and I'm planning for my future. It may or may not include remarriage someday, but I'm not living for the next chapter of my life because I'm enjoying this season very much.

We do not need to conform to what the world says "moving on" looks like because we can be very content with the life we have right now, just the way it is. Paul said he was content in all things, especially as a single man (Philippians 4:11). God wants us to learn to be content as single woman too.

Being Single Has Advantages

So I say to those who aren't married and to widows—it's better to stay unmarried, just as I am.

—1 Corinthians 7:8

We live in a couples-important society, yet more than half of the nation is made up of unmarried people. In 2015, the Bureau of Labor Statistics reported that more than 50 percent of Americans aged sixteen and up were single, not married. If so many of us are single, why does marriage define us? Why do we think that marriage will bring us happiness and completion that we don't already have?

First, let me say that dating or seeking out a man to be involved with—closely, even if not sexually—while you're still legally married is adultery. It doesn't matter if your divorce has been dragging on for years; as hard as it is, God intends for marriage to be honored no matter what the circumstances are. No matter if you're the only one not dating, until the divorced papers are signed and everything is finalized with an end date, you are still married in the eyes of God, as well as legally.

I knew my husband had a girlfriend (or girlfriends) while we were still married, but that didn't change my actions or intentions of honoring my marriage in front of God. By trusting God during this time, I walked out of my marriage with full integrity and no extra baggage of shame to carry. You shouldn't either.

Being single during this time—during and after divorce—is a gift, a gift from God to us. Every woman has the gift of singleness while she is unmarried. The gift gives us fewer distractions so we can find it easier to put God at the center of our lives. But when we don't experience singleness as a gift, we can experience discontentment and resentment instead. Take this time to get to know yourself and God more intimately by studying His Word and biblical history. Now you have more time to focus on learning all God would have you learn, and trusting Him with the path ahead.

He's trustworthy.

If God called you to divorce, or He chased away your unbelieving spouse, you can trust Him to show you why you should remain single during this time. You can also trust Him to let you know if you should remarry someday, after He's guided you through your healing.

Trust God to Guide You

> *Trust in the Lord with all your heart; do not depend on your own understanding. Seek his will in all you do, and he will show you which path to take.*

—Proverbs 3:5–6

For most of us, trusting anyone is an issue. I know that issue myself. But as God proves His love, you build back the trust lost during and after divorce.

As you experience difficulties and recall the previous times God has come through, you'll build faith that no matter the circumstances, God will be there and provide, just like He did for the Israelites.

When your faith starts to waver because of your circumstances, recall the women of faith of the Bible. Strong women who had faith that healed them instantly, women who were provided for after the death of a husband, women who were forgiven and then released from public stoning are all wonderful examples. Hebrews 11 showcases many more examples of faith in action throughout the entire Bible.

Although many stand out to me, the story of Rahab is one of my favorites. Her story is full of grace, mercy, strength, redemption and, more importantly, a life that acts in a manner that verifies faith is real. Rahab escaped destruction by having a strong faith and trusting in God. She was willing to surrender to God and did what was needed to continue God's story and fulfill His plan with her life. This was in spite of the fact that the world might have shamed her and said she didn't deserve such a position.

Draw on your faith, and the faith portrayed in the Bible, to keep ongoing confidence that no matter what happens, God is on your side. Fix your eyes on Jesus. Consider Christ, the ultimate example of faith, who gave His life for yours. Trust that your rewards are in heaven for continuing on in this race until you reach the prize.

> But we are not like those who turn away from God to their own destruction. We are the faithful ones, whose souls will be saved.
>
> —Hebrews 10:39

Having faith is being certain of the things you cannot see—like God's provision, God's protection, and God's redemption in your life. Surrender to His will for your life. He will make your paths straight.

The "Light" at the End of the Tunnel

> ...for the light makes everything visible. This is why it is said, "Awake, O sleeper, rise up from the dead, and Christ will give you light."
>
> —Ephesians 5:14

Surviving through the end of your marriage and the process of divorce is enduring destruction. Maybe your marriage itself was complete destruction from day one. Whatever the case, it's destruction you must get through to see God's purpose in all of it. You are reading this book because you needed to hear about my healing and to learn that there is a light at the end of this dark tunnel called destruction.

Jesus is the light we all need to see through the darkness and destruction to the brighter future ahead. Additionally, you must accept that there is no going back to what was. Remind yourself that the past is in the past for a reason while you keep moving forward. As you do so, use the mistakes of your past to guide you into a better future.

Once you have come to the place in your own healing where you no longer hemorrhage all over the place and don't feel as shaky about sharing your story, God will use you to speak life into those going through the same things you just went through.

Jesus healed for a purpose. Jesus told those whom He healed to spread the news of His miracles for the sole purpose of bringing more people to Him—saving many lives. God wants you to share your redemption story with someone so she can be healed as well. We can all help spread the light that is at the end of the tunnel.

Rebuild and Reclaim Your Life

You guide me with your counsel, leading me to a glorious destiny.

—Psalm 73:24

At some point in this journey, you'll start to find happiness and contentment in everyday life again. You'll have reclaimed your hope, healing, and faith through trials and triumphs while keeping your connection close with the One who gives us all hope. You'll care about yourself again and look at yourself through God's eyes. Your faith will be in the fact that God is making something beautiful.

You will have started to deal with your own issues and will have been there for your kids. You will be able to manage your stress and will have started to rebuild your family's home as you contribute as a team. There will be a time for you to build (or rebuild) a career that brings you fulfillment and purpose beyond being "Mom," or any other title. This is the time to invest in friendships that were limited during marriage. You have more time to bless others and build a life of ministry to others. God really wants us to live our best lives with what we have been given. He didn't take away our husbands to punish us but to reward us with a thriving life, as a daughter of a King.

What if God created you at such a time as this to experience everything you've experienced for a greater purpose? This is how we fulfill our destiny—by living out the life we've been given and seeking how to use it all for the kingdom of God. Whether you remarry or stay single for the rest of your life, God wants to use you and your gifts to save many lives. If you have to give up your purpose, the use of your God-given gifts, or your calling in order to enter another marriage, then that situation is not for you.

Use this time to rebuild and recreate your firm foundation in the Lord so you are able to be content in all things, now and in the future.

The road ahead is bright. Move on with

confidence that God is with you wherever you go. Jesus is our light that will never go dark. He said, "I am the light of the world. If you follow me, you won't have to walk in darkness, because you will have the light that leads to life" (John 8:12). He will guide you through the destruction; you just have to believe and keep the faith.

Final Thoughts

FAITH IS NOT ABOUT everything turning out okay; faith is about being okay no matter how things turn out. Divorce can bring us to our knees to beg God for a certain outcome, but what if that is not His plan? As hard as it is, we need to have faith enough to say, "Thy will be done, I will trust You," no matter the outcome.

One of the main things I had to decide was to move on no matter what happened or who left my life: move on in the sense that I had to put the past behind me, get healthy for myself and my child still at home, and go "no contact" with all the dysfunctional people that continued to try to purposely hurt me, even if I lost people in the process. Later, God showed me that His way was best even when it hurt my heart to put up protective boundaries.

Was that easy? No. Boundaries with toxic people never is. And since my divorce, two of my three children have decided they don't want be in my life because of my boundaries to protect my home and safe haven. They were never taught boundaries and don't understand that all relationships need them. That's hard to face and I can't say I like it, but I have to keep the faith that somewhere there is a plan, and this is certainly part of that plan. They have to learn things in their own time; all I can do is pray. Even if I don't get my prayers answered, I'm going to get healthy for me and for the legacy I leave behind, even if I'm not here to see it.

Our integrity is the only thing we take with us at the end of this life. We don't take our children, we don't take a spouse, and we all know we don't take material possessions, so keep the end in mind when troubles come your way or someone leaves your life. God is preparing you for what's ahead. "I don't mean to say that I have already achieved these things or that I have already reached perfection. But I press on to possess that perfection for which Christ Jesus first possessed me. No, dear brothers and sisters, I have not achieved it, but I focus on this one thing: Forgetting the past and looking forward to what lies ahead, I press on to reach the end of the race and receive the heavenly prize for which

God, through Christ Jesus, is calling us" (Philippians 3:12–14).

May God bless you in your healing journey.

About the Author

JEN GRICE is a full-time writer, speaker, life coach (who specializes in teaching boundaries), and entrepreneur, as well as a homeschool mom of one teenager. While building her online businesses, Jen completed her Bachelor of Science in Organizational Management with concentrations in psychology, sociology, and Bible studies. Jen's blog, started in 2011, has become her ministry since her divorce, which has been anointed by God to serve divorcing or divorced women in their healing journey. When she's not writing, she's educating herself and others in abuse and divorce recovery, watching real-life crime TV shows, or eating chocolate— preferably with salted caramel inside.

Jen believes that all Christian women can reclaim hope, find healing, live in peace, and live fully redeemed in Christ after divorce. She plans to write more books to help Christian women to embrace their lives, reclaim their power, and assert themselves in a way they can feel good about. What others had planned to use to hurt Jen, she plans to repurpose to save many lives. Genesis 50:20 and Psalms 107:2 are her favorite Bible verses.

Connect with Jen

WEBSITE   JenGrice.com
FACEBOOK facebook.com/jengriceauthor
TWITTER   twitter.com/jengrice_

DIVORCE & ABUSE HEALING
RESOURCES

JenGrice.com/Resources

HELP YOUR CHILDREN THROUGH
DIVORCE

http://jengrice.com/blog/help-children-through-divorce.html
(including books for them and you)

Acknowledgments

Special thanks to all of the ladies who donated so much of their time to this project. You helped me share, brand, and market the ministry God has given me—mentoring divorced Christian women. Thank you for using your gifts, time, and energy, and for sharing your wise wisdom so that I can give hope to the hurting.

Thanks to my reader team, Vicky, Michelle, LaToya, and of course my own Christian mentor, Sheila, for your honest feedback. I appreciate all of you!

Lastly, thanks to my publishing team of Sally at Inksnatcher and Jonathan at Jonlin Creative, who helped me to edit, wordsmith, typeset, and cover this book. I could not have done it and made it look so beautiful without you!

Made in the USA
Lexington, KY
16 August 2019